2024 GUIDE ON

STARTING A SUCCESSFUL

SMALL BUSINESS

Quick and easy step by step proven methods to follow on how to start, run, and grow your own business from scratch to develop your entrepreneurial spirit

Wayne White

TABLE OF CONTENTS

ABOUT THE BOOK   5

INTRODUCTION   13

CHAPTER 1   21

UNDERSTANDING ENTREPRENEURSHIP   21

CHAPTER 2   25

NAVIGATING SMALL BUSINESS LANDSCAPE   25

CHAPTER 3   29

BUILDING A SOLID BUSINESS PLAN   29

CHAPTER 4   33

LEGAL CONSIDERATIONS   33

CHAPTER 5   37

FUNDING YOUR VENTURE   37

CHAPTER 6   41

MARKETING STRATEGIES   41

CHAPTER 7   45

BUILDING A STRONG TEAM   **45**

CHAPTER 8   51

OVERCOMING CHALLENGES   **51**

CHAPTER 9   55

SCALING YOUR BUSINESS   **55**

CHAPTER 10   59

SUSTAINING SUCCESS   **59**

CHAPTER 11   63

REAL-LIFE SUCCESS STORIES: A TAPESTRY OF TRIUMPHS   **63**
A. ILLUMINATING ENTREPRENEURIAL JOURNEYS   63

CHAPTER 12   67

FREQUENTLY ASKED QUESTIONS   67

CONCLUSION   71

ABOUT THE BOOK

Welcome to Entrepreneurship

Embarking on the journey of entrepreneurship is like setting sail on uncharted waters. It's a thrilling adventure full of challenges and triumphs, and this guide is your compass in this vast entrepreneurial sea.

Overview of the Book's Approach

Unlike generic business guides, our approach is tailored for those dreaming of a thriving small business. We delve into practical strategies, real-life examples, and innovative solutions to make your journey not only successful but enjoyable.

How This Guide Will Benefit Aspiring Entrepreneurs

This guide isn't just a manual; it's a companion. Packed with insights, tips, and step-by-step instructions, it empowers you to turn your entrepreneurial vision into a reality. Let's explore the exciting world of small business together!

Understanding Entrepreneurship

Defining Entrepreneurship

At its core, entrepreneurship is the art of turning ideas into profitable ventures. We dissect this concept, exploring the mindset, skills, and passion that define successful entrepreneurs.

Importance in Today's Economy

In an era of constant change, entrepreneurship is the driving force behind economic growth. Discover why being an entrepreneur isn't just a career choice; it's a key player in shaping the future.

Characteristics of Successful Entrepreneurs

What sets successful entrepreneurs apart? We unveil the traits that make them stand out in the competitive business landscape.

Navigating Small Business Landscape

Identifying Opportunities

The first step in starting a successful small business is identifying opportunities. Learn how to spot gaps in the market and turn them into lucrative ventures.

Market Research and Analysis

Knowledge is power. Dive into the world of market research, understanding your audience, and analyzing competitors to give your business a competitive edge.

Crafting a Unique Value Proposition

In a crowded marketplace, standing out is crucial. We guide you through creating a unique value proposition that captures the attention of your target audience.

Building a Solid Business Plan

Importance of a Business Plan

A business plan is your roadmap to success. We break down its significance and guide you through crafting a comprehensive plan that aligns with your goals.

Key Components

From mission statements to financial projections, we detail each element of a robust business plan, ensuring your venture is built on a solid foundation.

Creating Realistic Financial Projections

Money matters. Explore the art of creating realistic financial projections that attract investors and help you manage your finances effectively.

Legal Considerations

Business Structure Options

Choosing the right business structure is crucial. We explore the options, from sole proprietorship to LLCs, guiding you toward the best fit for your venture.

Registering Your Business

Navigate the legalities of registering your business, ensuring compliance and setting the stage for a smooth launch.

Understanding Tax Obligations

Tax season shouldn't be daunting. We simplify the complexities of business taxes, helping you understand and fulfill your obligations.

Funding Your Venture

Exploring Funding Options

Funding is the lifeblood of any startup. We explore various funding options, from bootstrapping to seeking investors, helping you choose the right path for your business.

Pitching to Investors

Crafting a compelling pitch is an art. Learn the key elements that make investors sit up and take notice of your business.

Managing Finances Effectively

Money management is a skill every entrepreneur must master. We provide practical tips for managing your finances, ensuring long-term sustainability.

Marketing Strategies

Branding Your Business

Your brand is your identity. Discover the art of branding and how it can set the tone for your business in the market.

Online and Offline Marketing Tactics

In a digital age, online marketing is paramount. We also explore effective offline strategies, ensuring a well-rounded approach to reaching your audience.

Social Media Presence

Social media is a powerful tool. Learn how to leverage platforms to build a strong online presence and connect with your target audience.

Building a Strong Team

Importance of Team Dynamics

Behind every successful business is a strong team. Explore the dynamics of team building and creating a collaborative work environment.

Hiring the Right Talent

Your team is your biggest asset. Learn how to hire the right talent that aligns with your company culture and goals.

Fostering a Positive Work Culture

A positive work culture is the backbone of a thriving business. Discover strategies to cultivate a workplace where employees flourish.

Overcoming Challenges

Common Challenges in Small Businesses

Challenges are inevitable. We discuss common hurdles faced by small businesses and provide strategies for overcoming them.

Strategies for Overcoming Setbacks

Resilience is key. Explore strategies for bouncing back from setbacks, turning challenges into opportunities for growth.

- *Adapting to Changing Market Trends*
- *The business landscape is ever-evolving.*

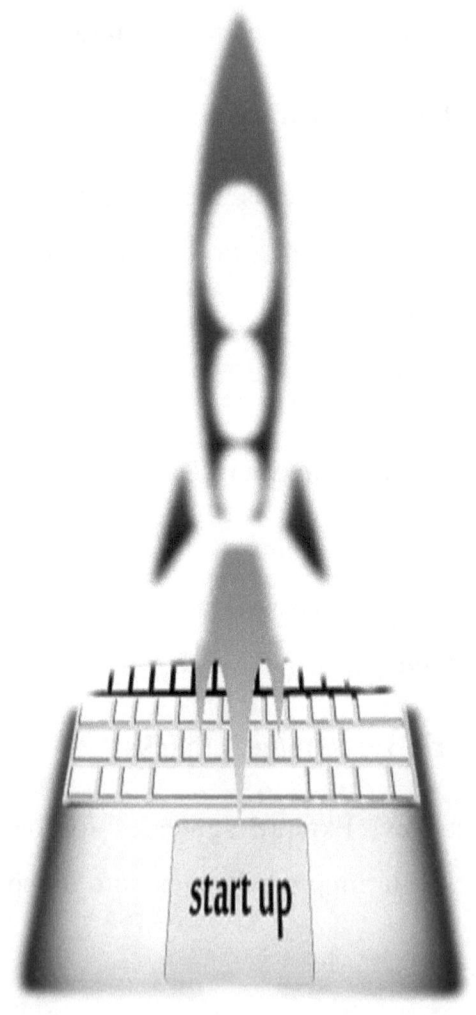

INTRODUCTION

"In the grand tapestry of business, opportunities are like stars in the night sky—countless, waiting to be discovered. And so was the story of Wayne White,

"As the saying goes, 'A single spark can start a prairie fire.' In the vast landscapes of entrepreneurship, so can a singular idea ignite a journey of limitless possibilities."

Greetings, fellow entrepreneurs and visionary minds,

Allow me to take you on a riveting journey—a journey that transcends the conventional bounds of business and delves into the heart of scaling, growth, and uncharted territories. I am Wayne White, an American entrepreneur who, much like many of you, embarked on the rollercoaster ride of starting and scaling a business.

Our story begins with a single spark—an idea that ignited the flame of possibility. Little did I know that this ember would evolve into a blaze, propelling my venture beyond the horizons I had envisioned. This book is not just a guide; it's a narrative infused with real experiences, pitfalls, and triumphs that mirror the entrepreneurial odyssey.

In the pursuit of scaling, I encountered challenges that felt insurmountable, from the common hurdles faced by small businesses to setbacks that tested the very core of my resilience. The pages that follow are not just filled with strategies and theories; they encapsulate the essence of overcoming, adapting, and thriving in a landscape that is as dynamic as it is unpredictable.

We'll explore the critical art of recognizing growth opportunities, drawing inspiration from moments in my own journey where seizing the right chance propelled my business forward. Diving into the intricacies of expanding your product or service line, we'll navigate the delicate balance between innovation and customer loyalty—a balance I've learned through trial, error, and triumphant successes.

And partnerships, ah, the symbiotic dance of collaboration. I'll share the stories of forging alliances that not only expanded my reach but fundamentally altered the trajectory of my business. Through strategic partnerships, I discovered that success isn't a solitary endeavor but a collective achievement.

So, join me on this expedition through the chapters of Scaling Beyond Horizons. Whether you're just setting foot on the entrepreneurial path or looking to elevate your established venture, this book is crafted for you. It's not just a manual; it's a companion—an exploration of possibilities that will resonate with your aspirations and equip you with the tools to conquer the peaks of business growth.

In the spirit of a single spark setting a prairie on fire, let's kindle the flames of innovation, resilience, and success. The journey awaits, fellow entrepreneurs—let's scale beyond horizons.

A. Welcome to Entrepreneurship

Embarking on the exhilarating journey of entrepreneurship is akin to setting sail on uncharted waters. As you stand on the precipice of innovation and independence, this guide extends a warm welcome, guiding you through the labyrinth of challenges and triumphs that define the entrepreneurial landscape.

B. Overview of the Book's Approach

Unlike generic business guides that offer one-size-fits-all solutions, our approach is bespoke, tailored specifically for the aspiring entrepreneur. Within these pages, you'll find a roadmap crafted with precision and care, providing not just instructions but a companionable hand to navigate the complexities of starting a successful small business.

C. Benefits for Aspiring Entrepreneurs

This guide isn't merely a compendium of information; it's a treasure trove of insights designed to benefit and empower those with the entrepreneurial spirit. Aspiring entrepreneurs can expect:

❖ **Practical Strategies:** Explore actionable strategies backed by real-world examples, ensuring that theoretical knowledge transforms into practical wisdom.

❖ **Step-by-Step Guidance**: Navigate each phase of entrepreneurship with confidence, as we break down the process into manageable, actionable steps.

❖ **Innovative Solutions**: Discover innovative solutions to common challenges, equipping you with the tools to approach problems with creativity and resilience.

❖ **Inspiration:** Immerse yourself in the stories of successful entrepreneurs, drawing inspiration from their journeys to fuel your own path to success.

❖ **Holistic Understanding**: Gain a comprehensive understanding of the multifaceted world of small business, covering everything from legal considerations to marketing strategies.

D. The Promise of Entrepreneurial Excellence

Our commitment extends beyond providing information. This guide promises:

- **Current and Relevant Content**: Stay abreast of the latest trends and best practices in the dynamic world of entrepreneurship, ensuring that the information you receive is both timely and relevant.

- **Interactive Learning:** Engage with the content through interactive elements, exercises, and case studies that reinforce key concepts and enhance your learning experience.

- **Community Support**: Join a community of like-minded individuals, where you can share experiences, seek advice, and forge valuable connections on your entrepreneurial journey.

- **Access to Additional Resources**: Unlock supplementary resources, tools, and templates to further facilitate your business planning and implementation.

As you turn the pages of this guide, envision it not just as a manual but as a trusted companion, propelling you towards entrepreneurial excellence. Whether you're a novice or seasoned entrepreneur, the benefits encapsulated within these chapters are poised to transform your aspirations into tangible achievements.

CHAPTER 1

Understanding Entrepreneurship

A. Defining Entrepreneurship

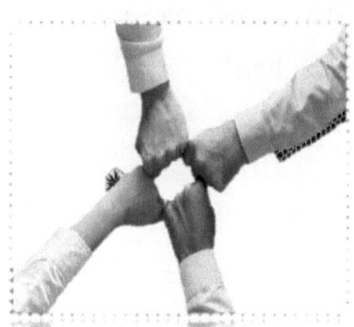

At the heart of every great venture lies the essence of entrepreneurship. In this section, we embark on a journey to unravel the multifaceted nature of entrepreneurship. It's more than a word; it's a mindset, a philosophy, and a way of life. We explore how entrepreneurs see opportunities where others see challenges, how they transform ideas into reality, and why being entrepreneurial is not just about starting businesses but about fostering innovation and driving positive change.

B. Importance in Today's Economy

In an era defined by rapid change and technological advancement, the role of entrepreneurship in shaping the economy has never been more critical. This segment navigates the intricate relationship between entrepreneurship and the contemporary economy. Entrepreneurs are the architects of progress, driving economic growth, creating jobs, and challenging the status quo. We delve into case studies of successful entrepreneurs who have not only disrupted industries but have also become pillars of economic sustainability.

Discover why entrepreneurship is a force multiplier in the economy, influencing everything from market dynamics to societal advancement. By understanding this symbiotic relationship, you'll gain a profound appreciation for the impact of entrepreneurship on the world stage.

C. Characteristics of Successful Entrepreneurs

What sets the titans of entrepreneurship apart from the rest? In this section, we unveil the enigmatic qualities that characterize successful entrepreneurs. It's more than just having a good idea; it's about possessing a unique set of traits that fuel the journey from ideation to realization.

> **Resilience**: Explore the stories of entrepreneurs who faced setbacks and challenges but emerged stronger. Resilience is the bedrock on which successful ventures are built.

> **Adaptability**: The business landscape is ever-changing. Successful entrepreneurs have a knack for not just surviving but thriving in the face of uncertainty.

> **Visionary Thinking**: Beyond the immediate challenges, entrepreneurs have a vision for the future. We delve into how cultivating a visionary mindset can be a game-changer.

> **Effective Leadership**: Successful entrepreneurship is often a team effort. Learn the art of leadership that inspires and motivates teams to achieve greatness.

> **Innovative Spirit**: Innovation is the lifeblood of entrepreneurship. Discover how successful entrepreneurs consistently bring fresh ideas and solutions to the table.

By examining these characteristics, you'll not only gain insights into the minds of successful entrepreneurs but also find inspiration to nurture these traits within yourself. The journey of entrepreneurship is as much about personal growth as it is about business success. This section serves as a compass, guiding you toward cultivating the qualities that will set you on the path to entrepreneurial triumph.

Chapter 2

Navigating Small Business Landscape

A. Identifying Opportunities

 In the dynamic world of small business, success often hinges on the ability to spot opportunities where others see obstacles.

This section serves as your guide to developing a keen entrepreneurial instinct for identifying untapped markets, emerging trends, and unmet customer needs. Through real-world examples and practical exercises, we'll nurture your capacity to turn challenges into opportunities and transform your business ideas into actionable plans .

Learn to see the potential in every situation, understand the needs of your target audience, and identify gaps in the market that can be filled with innovative solutions. This skill is not just about finding opportunities; it's about creating them.

B. Market Research and Analysis

Knowledge is the cornerstone of strategic decision-making in small business. In this section, we dive into the importance of thorough market research and analysis. You'll discover how to collect and interpret relevant data, understand market trends, and anticipate changes in consumer behavior. From conducting surveys to studying competitors, we provide a comprehensive toolkit to empower you with the insights needed to make informed and strategic choices for your small business.

This isn't just about gathering information for the sake of it; it's about understanding your market deeply, identifying your competitive advantages, and positioning your business for sustained success in a dynamic environment.

C. Crafting a Unique Value Proposition

In a world where choices abound, your business needs to stand out. Crafting a compelling value proposition is your ticket to differentiation. We guide you through the process of defining your brand identity, understanding what makes your product or service unique, and effectively communicating that uniqueness to your target audience.

This section goes beyond theory; it's a hands-on exploration of how to create a value proposition that resonates with your customers. We dissect successful examples, explore the psychology behind consumer decision-making, and provide practical tips to help you articulate why your small business is not just a choice but the best choice.

Your value proposition is not just a marketing tool; it's the soul of your business. By the end of this section, you'll have the skills to craft a narrative that not only attracts customers but also forms a lasting connection with them.

Your small business is unique, and this section equips you with the tools to showcase that uniqueness to the world. It's not just about surviving in the small business landscape; it's about thriving and leaving a lasting impact.

CHAPTER 3

Building a Solid Business Plan

In the intricate tapestry of entrepreneurship, a business plan is the compass that not only points the way but ensures a steady course amidst the ever-changing tides of the business world.

This section delves into the profound importance of a well-crafted business plan. It serves as the cornerstone of your entrepreneurial journey, providing a structured framework that aligns your goals, strategies, and actions. Beyond its role in securing funding, a business plan becomes your strategic ally, offering clarity in decision-making and resilience in the face of challenges.

Discover how a business plan becomes a dynamic document, adapting to the evolving needs of your business and positioning you for success in a competitive landscape.

B. Key Components

Crafting a business plan is an art, and like any masterpiece, it requires careful consideration of its key components. In this section, we dissect each element, offering a comprehensive guide to constructing a business plan that resonates with stakeholders. From the succinct yet impactful executive summary to the detailed market analysis and competitive landscape, we explore how each component contributes to the narrative of your business.

This is more than a checklist; it's a roadmap for creating a business plan that not only impresses but becomes a living document—one that guides and evolves with your business.

C. Creating Realistic Financial Projections

Numbers are the language of business, and financial projections tell a story of your venture's future. In this section, we demystify the often-intimidating process of creating realistic financial projections. From revenue forecasts to expense management, we provide actionable insights into developing financial models that not only capture the essence of your business but also instill confidence in potential investors.

Learn the delicate balance of optimism and pragmatism, projecting growth without overreaching, and presenting financial data that not only paints a realistic picture but also showcases the financial viability of your small business. Building a solid business plan is akin to constructing a sturdy foundation for a building. It ensures stability, resilience, and the capacity to weather storms.

This section is more than a guide; it's an invitation to transform your ideas into a tangible, strategic plan that not only attracts investment but sets the stage for the sustainable growth of your small business. It's time to turn visions into reality, and the business plan is your blueprint for success.

CHAPTER 4

Legal Considerations

In the realm of small business, the legal structure you choose is not just a formality; it's a strategic decision that impacts every facet of your operation.

This section takes you on a journey through various business structure options, each with its own set of advantages and considerations. Whether you're exploring the simplicity of a sole proprietorship, the liability protections of an LLC, or the scalability of a corporation, we provide insights that empower you to make a choice aligned with your business goals.

Unlock the knowledge needed to navigate the legal intricacies of business structures, ensuring that your choice lays a solid foundation for the growth and sustainability of your small business.

B. Registering Your Business

Transitioning from a conceptualized business to a legally recognized entity involves a crucial step: registration. This section is your guide to the intricacies of registering your business. From selecting a business name that reflects your brand to completing the necessary paperwork, we demystify the process. Understanding the legal obligations and benefits of registration is paramount. It not only establishes your business's legitimacy but also provides a shield against potential legal challenges while fostering trust among customers and partners.

By the end of this section, you'll not only have a registered business but also the confidence that comes with knowing your venture stands on a solid legal footing.

C. Understanding Tax Obligations

Taxes are a constant in the business landscape, and comprehending your obligations is essential for financial stability. In this section, we unravel the complexities of business taxes. Navigate through tax codes, discover available deductions, and learn about credits tailored for small businesses. We go beyond mere compliance, providing strategic insights into how your choice of business structure influences your tax liability.

Equip yourself with proactive strategies to not only meet tax obligations but also optimize your financial resources for the continued success of your small business. This section is not just about surviving tax season; it's about mastering the art of tax planning, ensuring that your business not only meets its legal responsibilities but also thrives in a tax-efficient manner.

Legal considerations are the invisible scaffolding that supports the visible success of your small business. This section isn't just a manual; it's your legal companion, offering guidance that empowers you to make informed decisions. As you navigate through the legal intricacies, remember: each decision is a stepping stone toward the resilience and longevity of your small business.

Chapter 5

Funding Your Venture

The path from a visionary idea to a flourishing business often requires the infusion of capital. In this section, we embark on a comprehensive exploration of the myriad funding options available to fuel your venture's growth. Whether you are considering traditional loans, venture capital, government grants, or exploring the possibilities of peer-to-peer lending, we provide an in-depth analysis of each avenue. Learn the nuances of each funding option, understand the associated risks and benefits, and gain insights into aligning your funding strategy with the unique needs and goals of your small business.

Navigate the financial landscape with confidence, armed with the knowledge to choose the funding options that best suit your business's trajectory and vision.

B. Pitching to Investors

Pitching your business to investors is an art form that goes beyond numbers and charts; it's a narrative that captures imagination and secures support. In this section, we delve into the intricacies of crafting a compelling pitch that resonates with potential investors. From refining your value proposition to constructing a persuasive presentation, we guide you through the elements that make a pitch successful.

Uncover the psychology of investor decision-making, learn to address concerns preemptively, and master the art of storytelling to leave a lasting impression. By the end of this section, you'll not only be a confident pitcher but also possess the skills to convey the unique value of your business, attracting the financial backing needed for growth.

C. Managing Finances Effectively

Financial acumen is the backbone of a thriving business. This section serves as your guide to effective financial management for your small business. From creating realistic budgets to monitoring cash flow and interpreting financial statements, we provide practical insights to ensure the financial health of your venture. Discover how to leverage financial tools, understand the significance of key performance indicators, and implement strategies that contribute to the sustained financial success of your small business.

Equip yourself with the skills to not only secure funding but also manage those funds strategically, ensuring that your financial decisions align with the overarching goals of your business. Funding your venture is not merely about acquiring resources; it's about strategically positioning your business for success. This section is your financial compass, guiding you through the diverse funding options, empowering you to craft persuasive pitches, and arming you with the financial management skills crucial for long-term sustainability. As you explore funding avenues and navigate financial landscapes, remember that each financial decision is a building block in the construction of a resilient and thriving small business.

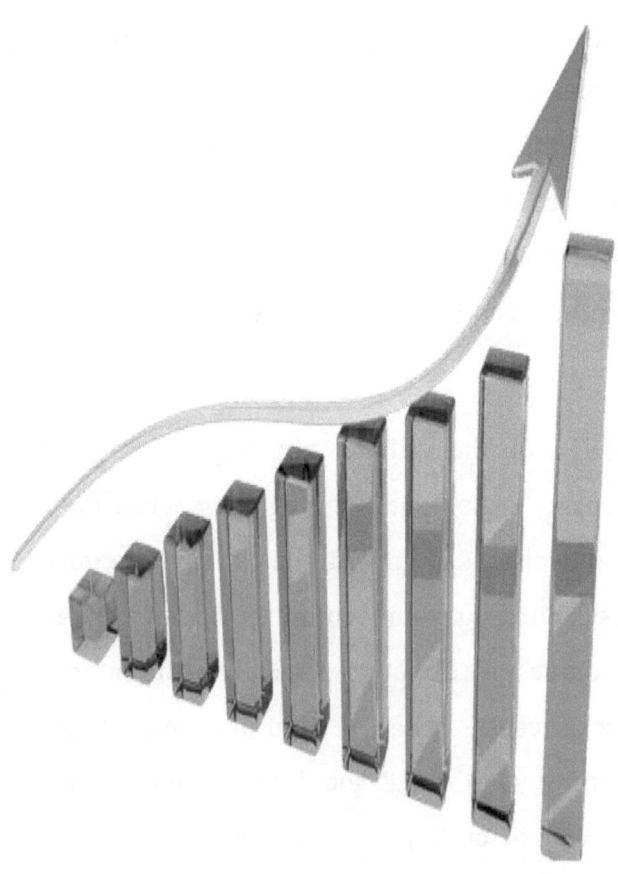

Chapter 6

Marketing Strategies

A. Branding Your Business

 Crafting a brand is an art, and in this section, we delve deeper into the subtleties that make your business memorable.

Beyond the visuals, we explore the emotional connection your brand creates. Understand the impact of a well-defined brand voice, how to communicate your values effectively, and why consistency is the linchpin of brand success. We unravel the psychology behind consumer loyalty and guide you in creating a brand that not only stands out but resonates with your audience on a profound level.

By the end of this section, you'll not only have a brand; you'll possess the tools to build a brand that becomes a trusted companion for your customers on their journey.

B. Online and Offline Marketing Tactics

The marketing landscape is a blend of digital and tangible strategies, and mastering both is a strategic imperative. This section is your comprehensive guide to navigating the complexities of online and offline marketing. Dive into the intricacies of SEO, explore the power of targeted online advertising, and understand how traditional methods, from event sponsorships to print advertising, can complement your digital efforts. We provide insights into crafting a seamless marketing strategy that maximizes visibility and impact across diverse channels.

This isn't just about choosing between online and offline; it's about creating a harmonious symphony that resonates with your audience wherever they are.

C. Social Media Presence

Social media isn't just a platform; it's a dynamic ecosystem where businesses thrive. In this section, we go beyond the basics, exploring advanced strategies for a robust social media presence. From harnessing the power of visual content to understanding the algorithms that govern each platform, we delve into the nuances. Discover how to create shareable content, build an engaged community, and use analytics to refine your approach. This section isn't just about having a presence; it's about making a meaningful impact in the crowded social media landscape.

By the end of this section, you'll not only be adept at navigating social media platforms, but you'll also have the skills to turn your social presence into a powerful engine for brand growth and customer engagement.

Marketing is not a static concept; it's a dynamic force that evolves with your business and the market. This section serves as your guide to not just understanding but mastering the ever-changing landscape of branding, online and offline tactics, and social media dynamics. As you implement your marketing strategies, remember that each interaction is an opportunity to create a lasting impression and solidify your brand's position in the hearts and minds of your audience.

Chapter 7

Building a Strong Team

A. Importance of Team Dynamics

In the fast-paced world of entrepreneurship, the importance of robust team dynamics cannot be overstated. Your team is not just a collection of individuals; it's a living organism that breathes life into your business. This section delves even deeper into the dynamics that make a team formidable. Explore the art of harnessing diverse strengths, fostering collaboration, and creating an environment where innovation is not just encouraged but thrives. From understanding the unique talents each team member brings to cultivating effective communication, discover the nuanced elements that contribute to a high-performing and harmonious team.

By the end of this section, you'll not only recognize the critical role of team dynamics but also possess the insights to actively nurture a team that not only supports your business goals but propels them to new heights.

B. Hiring the Right Talent

Building a strong team starts with selecting individuals who align not just with the roles but with the very ethos of your company. This section acts as your compass in the art of hiring the right talent. Dive into the intricacies of crafting job descriptions that attract the right candidates and conducting interviews that unveil not only technical skills but character and cultural fit. Learn to look beyond resumes and qualifications, tapping into the intangibles that make a candidate not just an employee but a cultural fit and valuable contributor to your overarching vision.

Uncover strategies to not only attract top-tier talent but to build a team that not only possesses the necessary skills but shares an intrinsic passion for the success of your business.

By the end of this section, you'll not only be adept at the hiring process but also understand the transformative impact the right team members can have on the growth, innovation, and sustainability of your business.

C. Fostering a Positive Work Culture

A positive work culture is the secret sauce that turns a group of individuals into a cohesive and high-performing team. This section is your comprehensive guide to cultivating a work environment where positivity is not just a buzzword but a guiding principle. From instilling a shared mission that aligns with your company values to fostering open lines of communication and recognizing achievements, we guide you through the steps to create a positive work culture. Understand how a motivated and engaged team translates into increased productivity, higher employee retention, and, ultimately, the success of your small business.

By the end of this section, you'll not only grasp the significance of a positive work culture but also possess the tools to actively cultivate an environment where your team not only excels but finds fulfillment in contributing to the success of your venture.

Building a strong team is a continuous journey that goes beyond the initial hiring process; it's about creating a collective force that evolves and adapts with your business. This section is your holistic guide to understanding the intricacies of team dynamics, refining your hiring strategies, and actively shaping a positive work culture. As you navigate the ongoing journey of building and sustaining your team, remember that each team member is a valuable asset contributing to the resilience, innovation, and long-term success of your business.

By the end of this section, you'll not only grasp the significance of a positive work culture but also possess the tools to cultivate an environment where your team not only excels but finds fulfillment in contributing to the success of your venture.

Building a strong team is an ongoing process that goes beyond hiring; it's about creating a collective force that aligns with your business goals. This section is your comprehensive guide to understanding the intricacies of team dynamics, hiring strategies, and work culture. As you navigate the journey of building and sustaining your team, remember that each team member is a valuable asset contributing to the resilience and success of your business.

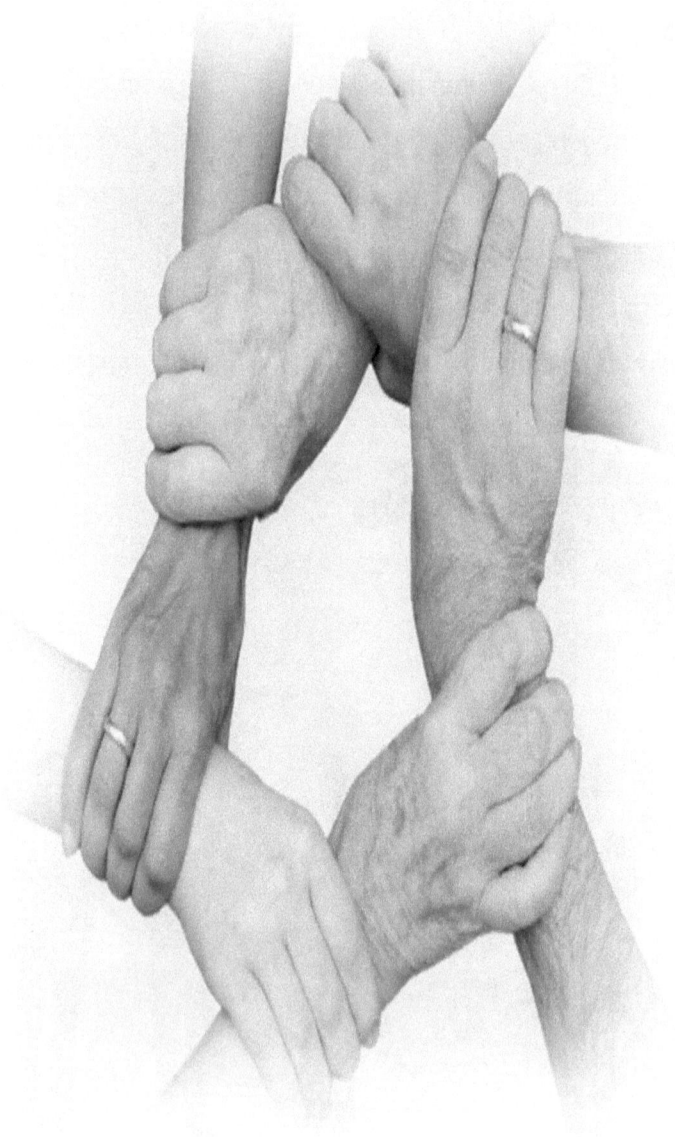

Chapter 8

Overcoming Challenges

A. Common Challenges in Small Businesses

In the intricate dance of entrepreneurship, challenges are not roadblocks but stepping stones to growth. This section illuminates the common challenges that often greet small businesses on their journey.

From navigating financial constraints and fierce market competition to addressing staffing issues and overcoming operational hurdles, we dissect each challenge. Gain a profound understanding of why these hurdles arise and, more importantly, equip yourself with strategic approaches to not only weather but conquer these challenges. Recognizing and anticipating these common pitfalls will empower you to navigate the intricate landscape of entrepreneurship with resilience and foresight.

By the end of this section, you'll not only identify the challenges but possess the insight to transform them into opportunities that propel the growth of your small business.

B. Strategies for Overcoming Setbacks

Setbacks are not the end of the road; they are pivotal moments for growth and innovation. This section is your guide to navigating the turbulent waters of setbacks with grace and strategy. Whether facing a financial downturn, recovering from a failed marketing campaign, or dealing with an unforeseen crisis, we explore actionable strategies to turn setbacks into catalysts for positive change.

Embrace a proactive mindset, learn to adapt swiftly to unexpected challenges, and cultivate resilience that transforms setbacks into stepping stones toward success. The strategies provided here are not just theoretical; they are pragmatic tools to empower you to navigate setbacks effectively and emerge stronger.

By the end of this section, you'll not only have a toolkit for overcoming setbacks but also a resilient mindset that views challenges as opportunities for transformative growth.

C. Adapting to Changing Market Trends

In the dynamic realm of business, adapting to changing market trends is not just a necessity; it's a strategic advantage. This section serves as your compass in understanding, embracing, and capitalizing on shifts in the market landscape. From the impact of technological advancements to the nuances of evolving consumer behavior, we explore the forces that drive change. Learn to not only anticipate market trends but also pivot your strategies effectively, positioning your small business as an agile and forward-thinking player in the market.

Discover how adaptability isn't just a survival skill but a proactive strategy that propels your business forward amid the ever-evolving market dynamics. By the end of this section, you'll not only recognize the significance of adapting to market trends but also have the practical tools to navigate change strategically, turning it into a competitive advantage for your small business.

Overcoming challenges is not merely a part of the entrepreneurial journey; it's the essence of growth and resilience. This section is your comprehensive guide to not only identifying common challenges but also developing the strategic mindset and practical skills needed to overcome setbacks and thrive in a dynamic business environment.

As you navigate the challenges ahead, remember that each obstacle is an opportunity to refine your strategies, fortify your business, and emerge victorious in the ever-evolving landscape of entrepreneurship.

Chapter 9

Scaling Your Business

A. Recognizing Growth Opportunities

 Scaling your business requires a discerning eye to identify and capitalize on growth opportunities.

In this section, we delve deeper into the art of recognizing avenues for expansion. Dive into the intricacies of market analysis, exploring not only current trends but also anticipating shifts on the horizon. Harness the power of customer feedback as a valuable compass pointing towards unmet needs and desires. Learn to conduct a comprehensive SWOT analysis to evaluate your business's scalability potential, understanding its strengths and areas for improvement.

By the end of this section, you'll not only be adept at spotting growth opportunities but also possess the strategic foresight needed to turn them into actionable plans for sustainable business growth.

B. Expanding Your Product/Service Line

Diversifying your product or service line is not just about offering more; it's about meeting evolving customer demands strategically. In this section, we dive into the intricacies of expanding your offerings. Explore the considerations involved in introducing new products or services, from analyzing market demand and competition to ensuring seamless integration with your brand identity.

Learn to navigate the delicate balance between innovation and maintaining the loyalty of your existing customer base. Understand how strategic expansion can not only attract new customers but also deepen relationships with your current clientele.

By the end of this section, you'll not only grasp the dynamics of product/service line expansion but also possess the skills to execute a comprehensive diversification strategy that propels your business forward.

C. Building Partnerships

Collaboration is the accelerant that can propel your business into new dimensions, and forming strategic partnerships is a key strategy for achieving this. In this section, we unveil the nuanced art of cultivating partnerships that foster growth. Explore the process of identifying potential collaborators, assessing their compatibility with your business goals, and negotiating agreements that benefit all parties involved.

Learn to go beyond transactional relationships, creating partnerships that offer access to new markets, shared resources, and complementary expertise. By the end of this section, you'll not only recognize the immense value of strategic partnerships but also possess the expertise to navigate the intricate landscape of collaboration, transforming it into a driving force for the sustained success of your business.

Scaling your business is a multifaceted endeavor, and this section serves as your in-depth guide to navigating the complexities of growth opportunities, product/service line expansion, and strategic partnerships. As you embark on the journey of scaling, remember that each strategic move isn't just a step towards growth but a pivotal moment in shaping the future success and resilience of your business in an ever-evolving market.

CHAPTER 10

Sustaining Success

In the turbulent seas of business, the compass that guides sustained success is unwavering customer satisfaction. This section navigates the intricacies of maintaining customer contentment. Dive into the strategies that create memorable customer experiences—personalized services, responsive communication, and a commitment to exceeding expectations. Learn the art of gathering and deciphering customer feedback, recognizing that a satisfied customer is not just a transaction but a long-term relationship. Understand the transformative power of customer-centric practices in building a business that stands resilient against the changing tides of the market.

By the end of this section, you'll not only understand the pivotal role of customer satisfaction but possess the tools to cultivate relationships that form the bedrock of your business's sustained success.

B. Innovating Your Business

Sustaining success is not a testament to stasis but an ode to perpetual innovation. This section is your manual for infusing innovation into the DNA of your business. Explore strategies to stay ahead, from adopting emerging technologies to fostering a culture of creativity within your team. Grasp the significance of market research and trend analysis, and learn how to implement changes that resonate with your evolving audience.

Realize that innovation is not confined to products or services but should permeate every facet of your business, ensuring continual relevance and resilience in a dynamic market.

By the end of this section, you'll not only advocate for innovation but also possess the skills to embed a spirit of continuous improvement into the fabric of your business.

C. Continuous Learning and Improvement

Sustained success is not a trophy; it's a journey marked by perpetual learning and improvement. In this section, we unravel the mindset and practices that uphold continual success. From fostering a culture of learning within your team to embracing personal and professional development, we guide you through the transformative steps. Learn the art of adapting to feedback, staying abreast of industry trends, and implementing changes that catalyze improvement.

Understand how resilience in the face of challenges and an unwavering commitment to ongoing learning position your business as a dynamic force in the market. By the end of this section, you'll not only grasp the essence of continuous learning but also possess the tools to nurture a culture of improvement, ensuring your business evolves as a resilient and adaptive entity in a dynamic business landscape.

Sustaining success is not a destination but a perpetual journey demanding attention, innovation, and an unwavering commitment to excellence. This section is your comprehensive guide, navigating you through the subtleties of maintaining customer satisfaction, infusing innovation, and fostering continuous learning and improvement. As you embark on the voyage of sustaining success, remember that each satisfied customer, innovative idea, and learning opportunity is a building block in the fortress of a business that not only thrives but endures.

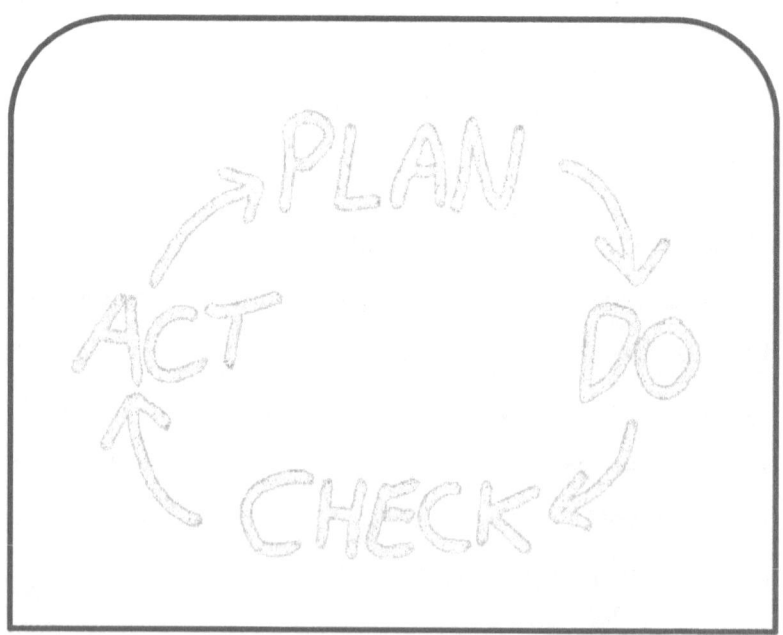

Chapter 11

Real-Life Success Stories: A Tapestry of Triumphs

A. Illuminating Entrepreneurial Journeys

 In the mosaic of entrepreneurship, each success story is a vibrant stroke that paints a narrative of resilience, innovation, and tenacity. This section unfolds as a gallery, showcasing diverse entrepreneurial journeys that echo the human spirit's capacity to transcend challenges. These narratives delve into the depths of adversity and emerge as beacons of inspiration for those navigating their own paths. From

bootstrap beginnings to disruptive innovations, these tales breathe life into the understanding that success is not a destination but a journey, marked by lessons, growth, and an unwavering commitment to one's vision.

By the conclusion of this section, you'll not only be captivated by these entrepreneurial odysseys but also glean insights into the myriad ways passion, perseverance, and adaptability intertwine to create lasting success.

B. Extracting Wisdom from Varied Experiences

In the complex terrain of entrepreneurship, learning from the rich tapestry of others' experiences is akin to acquiring a compass that guides your entrepreneurial voyage. This section navigates through a treasure trove of practical wisdom distilled from a spectrum of entrepreneurial encounters. From the stories of those who weathered economic storms to those who disrupted industries, the insights garnered provide a nuanced understanding of decision-making, risk mitigation, and strategic foresight.

Embracing the diverse experiences shared, you'll cultivate a multifaceted perspective, enriching your entrepreneurial toolkit with the collective wisdom of those who traversed similar paths.

As you conclude this section, you'll not only value the lessons woven into the fabric of these stories but also possess the analytical acumen to discern and apply these insights to your unique entrepreneurial journey.

C. Application of Lessons in Business Alchemy

The alchemy of knowledge transmutes into transformative power when applied to the crucible of real-world business challenges. This section serves as a crucible, facilitating the fusion of inspiration with strategic action. Dive into the art of applying lessons gleaned from the diverse array of entrepreneurial triumphs.

Learn to transmute the principles of resilience, adaptability, and visionary thinking into the operational DNA of your business. Identify the resonances between your entrepreneurial challenges and those surmounted by the trailblazers in these stories. Through this, you'll not only heighten your decision-making prowess but also forge a resilient business that stands impervious to the ebbs and flows of the market.

At the culmination of this section, you'll have not only absorbed the kaleidoscope of wisdom from these entrepreneurial chronicles but also acquired the adeptness to apply and tailor these lessons, turning them into catalysts for the success of your distinctive entrepreneurial journey.

In traversing these real-life success stories, envision them not merely as narratives but as guideposts lighting your way through the uncharted territories of entrepreneurship. Each story, each lesson, and each strategic application form an integral part of a roadmap, one that you craft as you navigate towards your own entrepreneurial triumph.

As you immerse yourself in this trove of experiences, remember that success is not just a destination; it's an ever-evolving journey, and the wisdom drawn from the experiences of others serves as a timeless compass, directing you toward your aspirations and beyond.

CHAPTER 12

Frequently Asked Questions

A. What are the first steps to starting a small business?

 Embarking on the journey of starting a small business is exhilarating, but it requires careful planning.

This FAQ explores the foundational steps that set the stage for success. Learn how to conceptualize a viable business idea, conduct thorough feasibility studies, navigate legal considerations, and choose a business structure that aligns with your goals. These initial steps lay the groundwork for a robust business foundation, ensuring that your entrepreneurial venture starts on solid footing.

B. How important is market research for a new business?

Market research is the bedrock of informed decision-making for a new business. In this FAQ, we delve into the critical importance of market research. Understand how market analysis not only identifies opportunities but also gauges competition and unveils customer needs. Gain insights into the role of effective market research in mitigating risks and positioning your business for strategic growth. This foundational knowledge empowers you to navigate the complexities of the market with confidence and agility.

C. What funding options are available for small businesses?

Securing adequate funding is often a pivotal challenge for small businesses. This FAQ serves as a guide to the myriad funding options available. Explore traditional avenues such as bank loans and government grants, and discover alternative sources like angel investors and crowdfunding.

Gain insights into tailoring your funding strategy to suit your business model, ensuring financial stability and sustainable growth. Navigating the funding landscape with a strategic approach is key to propelling your small business forward.

D. How do I create an effective marketing strategy?

Crafting a compelling marketing strategy is essential for the success of any small business. This FAQ provides actionable insights into creating an effective marketing plan. From defining your target audience and leveraging digital marketing tools to creating engaging content and measuring success, we guide you through the steps to build a strategy that not only attracts but captivates your audience. Discover the art of establishing a brand presence that resonates in a competitive market, setting your business apart.

E. What are the common pitfalls to avoid in entrepreneurship?

Entrepreneurship is a thrilling journey, but it comes with its share of challenges. This FAQ sheds light on the common pitfalls to avoid. From the importance of thorough market research and prudent financial management to recognizing the significance of scalability and building a robust team, we provide insights into navigating these challenges. Learn to anticipate and overcome these pitfalls with resilience and strategic foresight, ensuring that your entrepreneurial journey is characterized by success and sustained growth.

Frequently Asked Questions serve as a compass for aspiring entrepreneurs, providing valuable insights and guidance on the critical aspects of starting and growing a small business. As you step into the realm of entrepreneurship, these FAQs are designed to empower you with knowledge and strategic thinking, paving the way for a fulfilling and successful venture.

CONCLUSION

As we conclude this comprehensive guide to starting and growing a successful small business, let's recap the key takeaways that have been woven into the fabric of each section.

From the foundational steps of entrepreneurship to the nuances of sustaining success, you've explored a wealth of insights, strategies, and real-life stories. Embrace the lessons on market research, funding, marketing, and overcoming challenges. Recognize the importance of innovation, continuous learning, and the role of a robust team. These takeaways form the toolkit you need to navigate the intricate landscape of entrepreneurship.

B. Encouragement for Aspiring Entrepreneurs

To the aspiring entrepreneurs reading these pages, know that the journey you're embarking on is both challenging and immensely rewarding. The challenges are the crucible that refines your ideas, tests your resolve, and ultimately forges success. As you face obstacles, remember the lessons shared in real-life success stories and the FAQs that guide you away from common pitfalls. Embrace challenges as opportunities, setbacks as catalysts for growth, and each step forward as progress toward your goals. You have the resilience, creativity, and determination to transform your vision into reality.

C. Invitation to Begin the Journey

Now, equipped with knowledge, insights, and a roadmap for success, it's time to take that crucial first step. The invitation to begin your entrepreneurial journey is extended with open arms. Your ideas, your passion, and your unique perspective are the driving forces that will shape the success of your small business. The challenges you'll encounter are not roadblocks but stepping stones, and the lessons learned will be your guideposts. As you embark on this exciting adventure, remember that the journey itself is as valuable as the destination.

The world of entrepreneurship awaits your innovation, your resilience, and your unique contribution. Begin this journey not just with anticipation but with the confidence that you have the tools, insights, and inspiration to not only start but sustain and grow a successful small business.

Get ready to turn the page and commence your entrepreneurial odyssey. The possibilities are boundless, and the future is shaped by those bold enough to embark on this transformative journey.

Start Your Journey…..